Grandma
I want to hear your story

Section one
The Beginning

Section two
Family history

Section three
Childhood years

Section four
Teenage years

Section five
When I was..

Section six
Parenthood

Section seven
More about me!

Section eight
Final notes

The Life Graduate Publishing Group

No part of this book may be scanned, reproduced or distributed in any printed or electronic form without the prior permission of the author or publisher.

Copyright 2021 - The Life Graduate Publishing Group and Romney Nelson

We love to receive reviews from our customers. If you had the opportunity to provide a review we would greatly appreciate it.
Thank you!

A Place to Share My Life Memories.

Grandma xx

My Lifetime Legacy Journal

THE BEGINNING...

Baby Grandma

Grandma's Introduction

Before I start....just a brief introduction about me!

_____
_____
_____
_____
_____
_____
_____
_____
_____
_____

Name:

Signature

Date

THE BEGINNING......

Full Name at Birth

_____

Date of Birth   /   /
_____

Time of Birth   :
_____

Day of the week you were born?
_____

Height at birth? (if known)
_____

Weight at birth? (If known)
_____

Your Place of Birth (include the City/Town, Country)
_____

Did you have any siblings when you were born? If so, what were their names and their ages?

_____

_____

ADD ANY ADDITIONAL NOTES OR INFORMATION HERE...

THE BEGINNING.....

Share with us some information about your parents?

_____
_____
_____
_____
_____

Were you in good health as a baby?

_____
_____
_____

Did you have any unique characteristics or funny things you did as a baby?

_____
_____
_____
_____

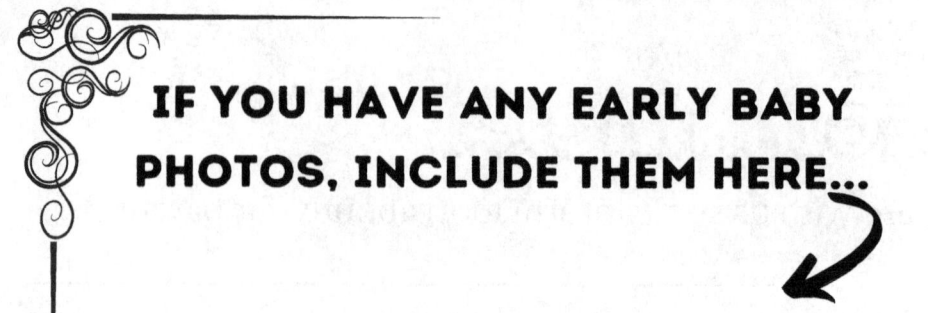

IF YOU HAVE ANY EARLY BABY PHOTOS, INCLUDE THEM HERE...

THE BEGINNING......

Were you an active or quiet baby?
_____
_____
_____
_____

Were you ever told what your first words were?
_____
_____

How old were you when you first walked?
_____
_____
_____
_____

THE BEGINNING.....

Can you remember what you loved to play as a toddler?

_____
_____
_____
_____

What is one of your earliest memories as a toddler?

_____
_____
_____
_____
_____
_____
_____
_____

THE BEGINNING.....

Were there any celebrations or birthdays you remember attending as a toddler?

_____

_____

_____

_____

Do you have a photo as a toddler you could include here?

THE BEGINNING. CONT...

Do you have any other memories or stories to share when you were a baby or toddler?

_____
_____
_____
_____
_____
_____
_____
_____
_____
_____
_____
_____
_____

"There is no influence so powerful as that of a mother."
—Sara Josepha Hale

FAMILY HISTORY

This is our Family Tree!

FAMILY HISTORY

My grandparents names were:

Grandmother (Fathers Side): _____

Grandfather (Fathers Side) _____

Grandmother (Mothers Side): _____

Grandfather (Mothers Side) _____

They were born in: (country)

Grandmother (Fathers Side): _____

Grandfather (Fathers Side) _____

Grandmother (Mothers Side): _____

Grandfather (Mothers Side) _____

This is something that not many people may know about our family history......

_____
_____
_____
_____
_____
_____
_____

Our FAMILY TREE

Grandfather

Grandfather

Grandmother

Grandmother

Mother

Father

Me

ADD ANY ADDITIONAL NOTES OR INFORMATION HERE ABOUT YOUR FAMILY HISTORY..

_____
_____
_____
_____
_____
_____
_____
_____
_____
_____
_____
_____
_____
_____
_____
_____
_____

CHILDHOOD YEARS

CHILDHOOD YEARS....

What was your favorite toy growing up?
___
___
___
___

Did you have a pet or any pets growing up?
___
___
___
___

What was your favorite T.V show to watch as a child?
___
___
___
___

Was there a moment you remember getting into big trouble as a child? Was there a punishment?

_____

_____

_____

_____

_____

Do you remember attending a special celebration or event that was very special to you?

_____

_____

_____

_____

_____

_____

_____

ADD ANY ADDITIONAL NOTES OR INFORMATION HERE...

CHILDHOOD YEARS....

What are your fondest memories growing up between the ages of 5 - 12 years?

_____
_____
_____
_____
_____
_____
_____
_____
_____
_____
_____
_____
_____
_____
_____

IF YOU HAVE ANY EARLY CHILDHOOD PHOTOS, PLACE THEM HERE...

CHILDHOOD YEARS....

What was your favorite meal as a child?

_____

What elementary/primary school did you attend and where was it located?

_____

_____

Describe your most memorable moment or story from elementary/primary school.

_____
_____
_____
_____
_____
_____
_____
_____

CHILDHOOD YEARS....

Where did you grow up as a child?
(house, location, town etc)

_____
_____
_____
_____

Who was your best friend or your best friends as a child?

_____
_____

What was your favorite day of the week and why?

_____
_____
_____
_____
_____

DO YOU HAVE ANY OR OTHER DETAILS TO SHARE?

_____
_____
_____
_____
_____
_____
_____
_____
_____
_____
_____
_____
_____
_____
_____

DO YOU HAVE ANY SCHOOL PHOTOS YOU CAN INCLUDE HERE?

TEENAGE YEARS

TEENAGE YEARS....

Describe your dress sense and clothing as a teenager. Is there anything that stands out for you?

_____
_____
_____
_____

Who taught you how to drive?

_____
_____
_____
_____

When and where did you learn to drive a vehicle?

_____
_____
_____
_____

TEENAGE YEARS....

What was your first vehicle and how much did you purchase it for? Tell us your special 'first car' story!

INCLUE ANY 'FIRST VEHICLE' PHOTOS OR OTHER INFORMATION HERE...

TEENAGE YEARS....

What High School did you attend and where was it located?

_____
_____
_____
_____
_____

Who was you favorite teacher or coach and why?

_____
_____
_____
_____
_____
_____
_____
_____

What was your favorite subject at school?

___

Did you date anyone at High School? If so, tell us a story about it.

___

SHARE ANY FURTHER DETAILS HERE

TEENAGE YEARS....

What hobbies did you have as a teenager?

_____
_____
_____

What is your most memorable moment as a teenager?

_____
_____
_____
_____
_____

If you knew what you know today, what would you have done differently as a teenager?

_____
_____
_____
_____
_____

SHARE ANY HIGH SCHOOL PHOTOS OR OTHER MEMORIES TO SHARE?

TEENAGE YEARS....

Did you have a close friendship group? Have you maintained contact with any of them?

_____
_____
_____
_____
_____
_____

Did you have any nicknames at High School?

_____
_____

What 5 words come to mind to describe your teenage years?

1. _____
2. _____
3. _____
4. _____
5. _____

WHEN I WAS..

WHEN I WAS....

When I was a child, my mode of transport to school was..
_____
_____

When I was in my teens, the biggest news story that I recall was .....
_____
_____
_____

When I was growing up, my 3 favorite movies were:

1. _____
2. _____
3. _____

WHEN I WAS....

When I was a child, the first movie I went to the theatre to see was..

_____

When I graduated from elementary/primary school, the year was.. _____

When I was a child, I wanted to be a......

_____

When I was 18 years old, my favorite music and band was..

_____

When I was in my teens, the most popular thing to do on a Saturday night was.......

_____

_____

When I was young, I loved to travel to.......

_____

_____

_____

WHEN I WAS....

When I graduated from school, I celebrated by...
_____
_____
_____
_____
_____
_____

When I was a teenager, the one thing I wish I had attempted to do was....
_____
_____
_____
_____
_____
_____
_____
_____
_____

USE THE NEXT 2 PAGES TO SHARE SOME TRAVEL PHOTOS

PARENTHOOD

PARENTHOOD....

How old were you when you first became a parent?

_____

Explain how you felt emotionally when you became a mother?

_____
_____
_____
_____
_____
_____
_____

Where were you located (city/town/country) when you had your first child?

_____
_____
_____
_____

SHARE SOME PARENTING PHOTOS HERE..

PARENTHOOD....

What has been the biggest challenge for you as a parent?
_____
_____
_____
_____
_____
_____

What are 3 key responsibilities you believe are important as a parent?

1 _____

2 _____

3 _____

PARENTHOOD....

When did you first become a grandparent? Share some information about when you became a grandparent.

_____
_____
_____

Share a special grandparenting story

_____
_____
_____
_____
_____
_____
_____
_____
_____
_____
_____

PARENTHOOD....

EXPAND ON ANY FURTHER PARENTING MEMORIES YOU MAY LIKE TO SHARE

MORE ABOUT ME!

ME TIME..

MORE ABOUT ME....

Not many people know this about me, so let me share it with you:

_____
_____
_____
_____
_____
_____

The activity or hobby that I enjoy most to do now is.....

_____
_____

I have the unique ability to be able to....

_____
_____
_____

MORE ABOUT ME....

If I was able to go back to a special time in history, it would be...

_____

_____

_____

If I could pass on some of advice to others, it would be..

_____

_____

_____

There are special moments in life that you wish you could pause to enjoy for longer. Mine would be......

_____

_____

_____

_____

_____

MORE ABOUT ME....

I wish I had the opportunity to...

_____

_____

_____

The quote that resonates most with me is..

_____

_____

_____

My favorite book of all time is:

_____

If there is one thing I would like to be remembered for it would be:

_____

_____

_____

_____

MORE ABOUT ME....

In no particular order, these are some of my most proudest moments:

_____
_____
_____
_____
_____
_____
_____
_____
_____
_____
_____
_____
_____

MORE ABOUT ME....

MORE ABOUT ME....

My SUPER-POWER is the ability to.....

_____

_____

_____

_____

If there were 3 famous people that I could invite for dinner, they would be:

1 _____

2 _____

3 _____

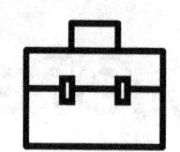

MORE ABOUT ME....

From my teen years, these are the jobs that I've had:

_____
_____
_____
_____
_____
_____
_____
_____
_____
_____
_____
_____

MORE ABOUT ME....

One of the jobs that stands out as my most enjoyable has been..

_____

_____

The most interesting place I have ever traveled to has been.... (include the year/date this occurred)

_____

_____

_____

If I was given a free return flight to anywhere in the world, I would visit...(include your 'Why')

_____

_____

_____

_____

MORE ABOUT ME....

If I was granted 3 wishes, I would wish for....

_____

_____

_____

_____

_____

If someone wrote a book about my life, the title of the book would be.....

SOME EXTRA SPACE FOR MORE INFORMATION OR PHOTOS HERE..

SOME EXTRA SPACE FOR MORE INFORMATION OR PHOTOS HERE..

FINAL NOTES

FINAL NOTES.....

There have been many questions that I have answered in this book, but I would also like to share this with you...

Your time to write anything else you wish to share...

FINAL NOTES....

FINAL NOTES....

FINAL NOTES....

USE THE FOLLOWING PAGES FOR CERTIFICATES, AWARDS. PHOTO'S ETC..

THANK YOU FOR SHARING YOUR LIFE STORY

This book was created by
Romney Nelson

Book Review

JUST A REMINDER THAT IF YOU HAD THE OPPORTUNITY OF PROVIDING A REVIEW ON AMAZON IT WOULD BE GREATLY APPRECIATED. THANK YOU!

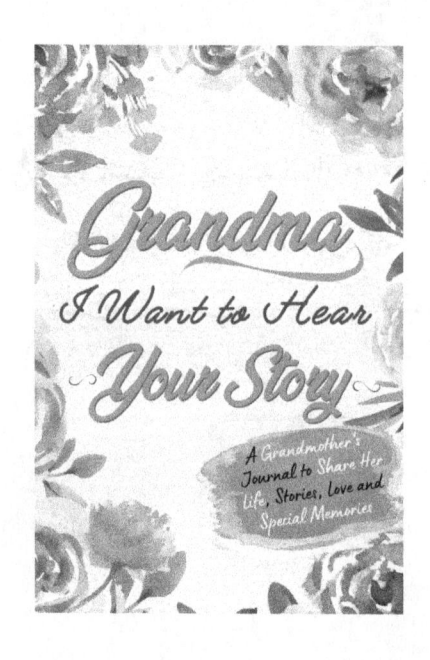

OTHER BOOKS
By
The Life Graduate Publishing Group

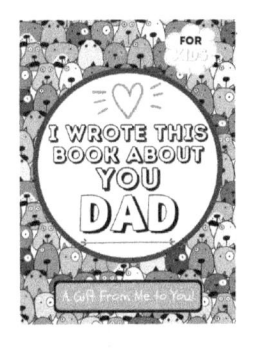

CPSIA information can be obtained
at www.ICGtesting.com
Printed in the USA
LVHW080150140621
690151LV00002B/20